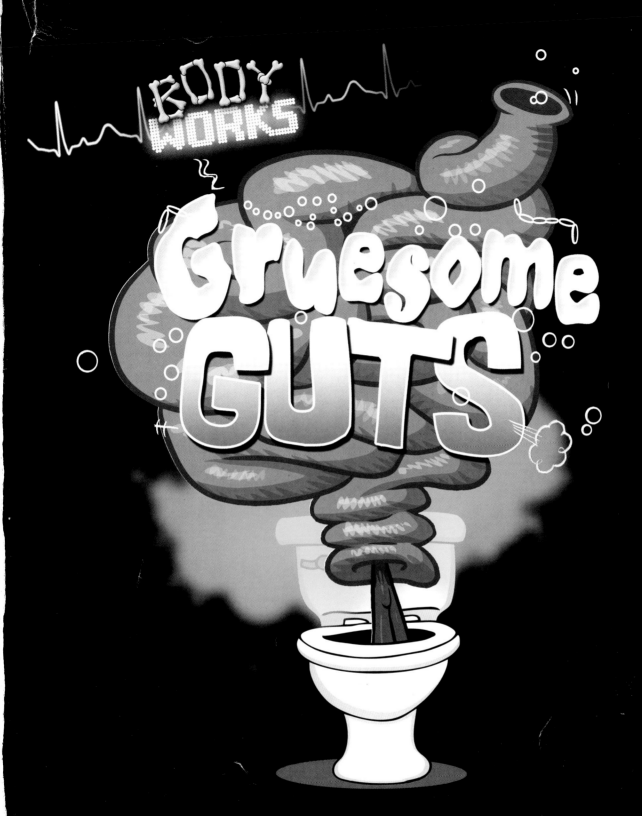

BODY WORKS

Gruesome GUTS

Anna Claybourne

QED Publishing

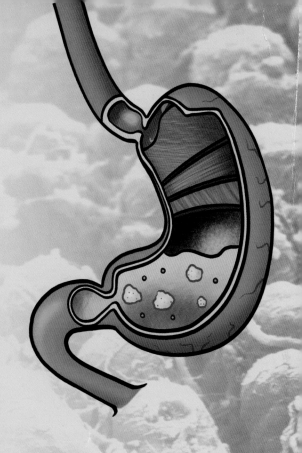

Created for QED Publishing by Tall Tree Ltd
Editor: Rob Colson
Designer: Jonathan Vipond
Illustrations, activities: Peter Bull
Illustrations, cartoons: Bill Greenhead

Copyright © QED Publishing 2013

Project editor for QED: Ruth Symons

First published in the UK in 2013 by
QED Publishing
A Quarto Group company
226 City Road
London EC1V 2TT

www.qed-publishing.co.uk

A catalogue record for this book is available from the British
Library.

ISBN 978 1 78171 118 7

Printed in China

Picture credits
(t=top, b=bottom, l=left, r=right, c=centre,)
Creative Commons: 21b Stell98; **Dreamstime**: 11b Ron Sumners;
Science Photo Library: 5b Claus Lunau, 11t David M Martin,
4–5, 15 Eye of Science, 15t, 17t Science Photo Library, 21 Garry
Watson; **Shutterstock**: 5t Steve Byland, 7t Ana Blazic Pavlovic,
8l Danny Smythe, 8r Alex Staroseltsev, 9tl Alexandr Makarov, 9b
Jesse Kunerth, 17b Ivonne Wierink, 19 Gelpi JM, 22b LianeM,
22–23 ifong, 23t Gtranquillity, 24–25 Gruffi, 25b Africa Studio,
26 Juan Gaertner, 27t Shutterstock, 27b Juan Gaertner,
29 Pressmaster

Note
In preparation of this book, all due care has been
exercised with regard to the activities and advice
depicted. The publishers regret that they can accept
no liability for any loss or injury sustained.

Words in **bold** are explained
in the Glossary on page 31.

CONTENTS

WHAT ARE GUTS FOR?

Have you ever thought about exactly what happens to your food? When you munch a mouthful of pizza or slurp on an ice cream, it's just the start of an amazing journey.

Whatever you eat is squeezed through a long series of tubes, chambers and narrow gaps that lead all the way through your body. Together, they are called the **digestive system**.

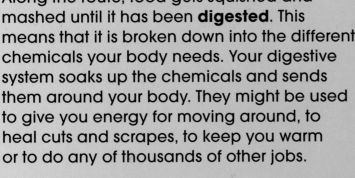

SQUEE-EEZE!

How does food move along inside your digestive system? Gravity helps, but your body also has another method, called 'peristalsis'. The oesophagus and guts have rings of strong **muscle** around them. The rings squeeze behind each lump of food to push it along.

Food processing

Along the route, food gets squished and mashed until it has been **digested**. This means that it is broken down into the different chemicals your body needs. Your digestive system soaks up the chemicals and sends them around your body. They might be used to give you energy for moving around, to heal cuts and scrapes, to keep you warm or to do any of thousands of other jobs.

Mouth

Throat

Oesophagus

Stomach

Intestines (also called the guts)

IMAGINE THIS...

In space, there is no gravity to help you swallow. That's fine for us, as we can rely on peristalsis. But birds would not survive for long. They need gravity to get food down their oesophagus and into their stomach.

GUTCAM

To take a look at your guts, doctors can give you a tiny device the size of a pill to swallow. This is called an endoscopic capsule, or 'gutcam'. It takes pictures of your insides and beams them back to a computer outside your body. The capsule travels through the whole digestive system, then leaves the body in your poo.

Endoscopic capsule travelling through the intestine.

5

DOWN THE HATCH!

MUSH IT UP!

Your digestive system begins with your mouth, which is a grinding, drooling and mushing machine. It transforms your food from crunchy or chewy morsels into a soft, gloopy mess, ready to be swallowed. To do this, all the parts of your mouth work together.

Your teeth crush and break up food into tiny bits.

Your mouth releases saliva, or spit, which mixes with the food, softens it and starts to **dissolve** it.

Salivary gland

Tongue

Epiglottis

To swallow your food, muscles in your throat squeeze the food balls into the oesophagus, which leads to the stomach.

Throat

Your tongue moves food around to make sure that every bit gets properly chewed. Then it rolls lumps of food into balls and pushes them to the back of your mouth.

Oesophagus

Windpipe

Food ball

SLOBBERY MOUTH

We think of saliva as something quite disgusting, but it's incredibly useful stuff. Besides making food soft and mushy, it contains germ-killing chemicals. It is also very slippery, and helps food to slide down your throat. Every day, the saliva glands in your mouth gush out about one LITRE of the stuff – enough to fill a large juice carton!

Babies often dribble lots of saliva, but when you're older this is considered very rude!

OPEN WIDE!

Incisors
Cutting teeth

Canines
Stabbing and holding teeth

Molars and pre-molars
Grinding and chewing teeth

CHOKING

Food or liquid sometimes 'goes down the wrong way'. This happens because your oesophagus is right next to your windpipe, the tube you use to breathe air. Normally, when you swallow, a flap called the epiglottis closes off the top of the windpipe. But if you try to eat while breathing in, or while laughing, food can slip down your windpipe by accident. If this happens, it makes you choke so that you cough the food back up.

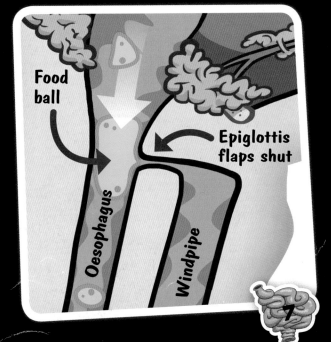

Food ball

Epiglottis flaps shut

Oesophagus

Windpipe

SLIPPERY SALIVA

You need saliva to help you chew, taste and swallow your food. Do these two tests to see the difference saliva makes.

YOU WILL NEED:

- Crackers or breadsticks
- Clock, stopwatch or timer
- Notebook and pencil
- Kitchen roll
- Ready-salted crisps

SLIMY SPIT

1 Break off two pieces of cracker or breadstick that are exactly the same size. Eat one, and time how long it takes to chew and swallow it (don't rush!). Write down the answer.

RESULTS

	With saliva	Without saliva
Cracker	8 seconds	

2 Use a piece of kitchen roll to dry your tongue and the inside of your mouth all over. Now eat the other piece of food, and time how long it takes to chew and swallow it.

It is impossible to eat more than two or three dry crackers in a row. They soak up so much saliva that your mouth can't make enough to keep up, and swallowing becomes impossible.

TASTY SALIVA

1 For your next experiment, stick your tongue out and place a crisp on it. Can you taste it? Write down what you can sense on your tongue.

2 Use kitchen roll to dry your mouth and tongue again. Then take a new, fresh crisp and repeat the test. What can you taste this time?

RESULTS

	With saliva	Without saliva
Ready-salted crisp	salty taste	

Your tongue can only taste food if it is wet.

What is happening?

Saliva makes food easier to mush up and helps it slide down your throat. That's why you can't swallow without it.

It also washes some of your food into your taste buds. These are found in tiny gaps between the bumps on your tongue. Without saliva, food doesn't wash into the gaps and you can't taste anything.

THE STRETCHY, SQUISHY STOMACH

When food reaches the bottom of your oesophagus, it moves into your stomach.

People often use the word 'stomach' (or 'tummy') to mean the front of the **abdomen**. But the real stomach is actually a large, bag-shaped **organ** that's a major part of your digestive system. It sits quite high up inside your body, on the left-hand side.

Strong muscles squeeze, churn and roll food around. This helps to mix it with the juices made in the stomach.

The juices in the stomach contain strong acid – a type of chemical that is good at dissolving other substances. As chunks and lumps of food sit in the acid, they gradually dissolve and turn into a liquid.

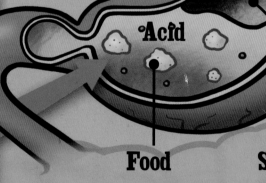

Oesophagus

Stomach

Muscles

Acid

Food

Stomach lining

FULL UP!

When you've just eaten a massive meal, how do you still have space for pudding? The answer is that the stomach is super-stretchy. It gets bigger as you stuff more food into it. The wrinkles in the lining of the stomach can stretch out, which allows it to expand from the size of a fist when empty to bigger than a melon when completely full.

Wrinkles in the stomach lining allow it to stretch when you eat.

BUUURP!

Burps happen when you swallow air or gas like the bubbles in fizzy drinks. The air bubbles out of your stomach, up the oesophagus and back out of your mouth.

DISGUSTING VOMIT!

When you throw up, the stomach squeezes very hard to force its contents back out through your mouth. It does this to get rid of germs or poison when you've eaten something bad. Some of the stomach acid comes out too – and that's why vomit is so stinky and revolting.

MODEL STOMACH

Your stomach is basically a bag full of acid and food. You can use simple household objects and ingredients to make your own model stomach.

YOU WILL NEED:

- Two small plastic bags with zip closures
- Vinegar
- Small beaker or teacup
- Cream crackers or other hard, dry crackers (not crumbly ones)
- Water

1 Put a small cupful of water into one bag. Put the same amount of vinegar into the second bag.

2 Break up a cracker into pieces. This represents how the cracker might be after you've chewed it. Put the pieces into the bag with the water and seal the bag. Now break up a second cracker. Put the pieces into the bag with the vinegar and seal the bag.

3 Leave the two bags for a few minutes for the liquid to soak in. Then pick up each bag in turn, and squish it to represent the action of the stomach muscles. Is one bag better at dissolving the cracker than the other?

4 Now try this with one broken cracker and one whole cracker. This will show you if chewing food before you swallow helps the stomach to dissolve it faster. Try out other food, such as boiled or chewy sweets, a banana, cheese or cereal.

What is happening?

Like the liquid in your stomach, vinegar is an acid. It is good at dissolving food and breaking it down. The cracker in the vinegar dissolves more quickly than the one in the water. Water is not acidic, and dissolves things more slowly.

Why doesn't your stomach eat itself?

The acid in your stomach can break down all kinds of food, including meat, which is made of muscle just like the stomach. But the stomach itself isn't dissolved. That's because its lining releases a thick, slimy goo that coats it all over, protecting it from the acid.

THE SMALL INTESTINE

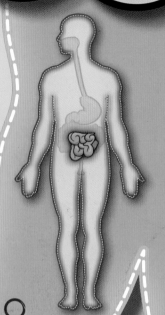

At the bottom end of your stomach is a narrow ring of muscle called the pyloric sphincter. Once food in the stomach has been turned into a mushy liquid, it squirts through this sphincter, and on to the next stage of its journey – your small **intestine**.

Pyloric sphincter

Small intestine

What's it for?

The small intestine is one of the most important parts of the digestive system. It contains substances called **enzymes** that break food down into useful **nutrients**, or food chemicals. As the nutrients flow along the small intestine, they are soaked up through its walls and into the blood.

Villi

Muscles
to push food along

Lining

The small intestine is lined with millions of tiny finger shapes, called villi. Nutrients pass through the thin walls of the villi into **blood vessels** inside them. The blood carries the nutrients around the body to the places where they are needed.

LONG AND LOOPY

The 'small' intestine is a strange name for this body part, as it's actually very long. It's a narrow tube about 3 cm wide, but in a typical adult, it measures around 6 m in length. The small intestine has to be long to give it enough time to do its job. By the time food finally gets to the end, most of the useful nutrients in it have been digested. If the small intestine were shorter, it wouldn't have time to catch all the nutrients.

To fit inside your body, the small intestine is coiled up into a series of folds and loops, as shown in this X-ray.

IMAGINE THIS...

A typical adult has about 4 million villi in their small intestine. The villi stick out, and this increases the surface area inside the intestine. If the whole surface could be flattened out, it would be the size of a tennis court!

THE LARGE INTESTINE

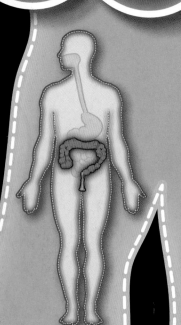

Your large intestine follows on from your small intestine. It's much shorter than the small intestine, but also wider and chunkier, which is why it's called the 'large' intestine.

The large intestine loops around the abdomen, surrounding the neatly coiled-up small intestine. It looks like a big, brown lumpy sausage.

Large intestine

What's it made of?

The large intestine is basically a big, rubbery tube of muscle. It has a slippery lining on the inside that allows food to move smoothly through it.

Food moves around the large intestine in a clockwise direction.

End of the small intestine

Appendix

Cecum

Rectum

The worm-shaped appendix sticks out from the cecum at the start of the large intestine.

Near the start of the large intestine is a strange little finger-sized tube called the appendix. Scientists once thought the appendix had no use. They now think it might be a storage place for helpful **bacteria** and chemicals that help the body to fight diseases.

THE LARGE INTESTINE'S JOB

Food sludge squeezes into the large intestine from the small intestine. The large intestine sucks water out of it, along with some salty chemicals, and carries them away into your blood. This is a slow job, and food spends 12 hours or more trundling through the large intestine.

LUMPY LEFTOVERS

The large intestine collects leftover food that your body can't digest – such as vegetable skins, seeds and pips. This is called dietary fibre. Your body can't break it down to use, but it's still important as it sweeps through your guts and keeps them clean. As the leftovers dry, they form into solid lumps – your poo!

MEASURE YOUR GUTS

The food that you eat goes on a long, winding journey through your body. If you could unwind your digestive system and lay it out, it would be almost as long as a classroom! To find out how long yours is, try this stringy gut activity.

YOU WILL NEED:

- Large ball of string
- Tape measure
- Calculator
- Scissors
- Sticky labels
- Pen
- A large floor area!

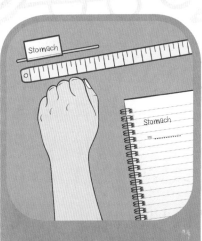

1 Make a fist and measure how wide it is. Multiply by 2 to find the length of your mouth and throat. Cut a piece of string this long. Wrap a label around the string and write 'mouth and throat' on the label.

2 Your oesophagus is about the length of your hand span – the distance from your thumb to your little finger when you stretch out your hand. Cut a piece of string this long and label it 'oesophagus'.

3 Just before you eat, your stomach is about the size and width of one fist. Cut a piece of string this long and label it 'stomach'.

4 The length of your small intestine is just over 3 times your full height. Measure how tall you are. Multiply this by 3.5 and cut a piece of string that long. Label it 'small intestine'.

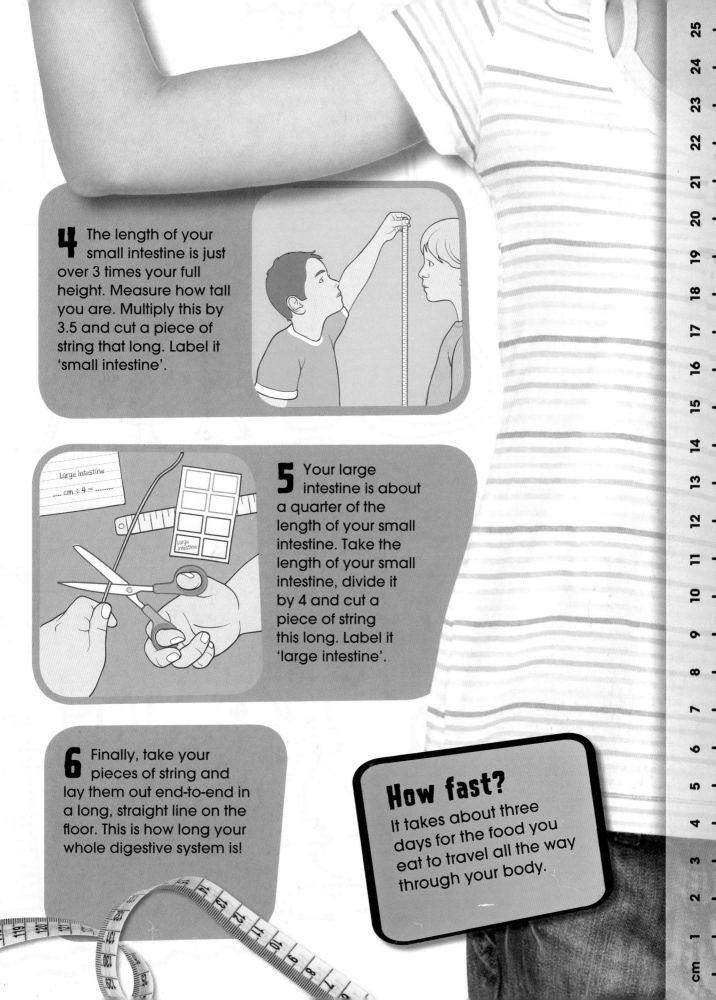

Large intestine
..... cm ÷ 4 = ...

Large
intestine

5 Your large intestine is about a quarter of the length of your small intestine. Take the length of your small intestine, divide it by 4 and cut a piece of string this long. Label it 'large intestine'.

6 Finally, take your pieces of string and lay them out end-to-end in a long, straight line on the floor. This is how long your whole digestive system is!

How fast?

It takes about three days for the food you eat to travel all the way through your body.

HELPING OUT

The digestive system is mainly a series of tubes that food passes through. But other organs also play an important part in digestion, even though food does not go through them.

Liver

BLADDER OF BILE

The gall bladder is next to the stomach. It holds a very strong, greenish-yellow substance called bile, which is good at breaking down fatty food. When you eat something fatty, such as chips, cheese or a cream cake, the gall bladder releases bile into the small intestine to help digest it.

Stomach

Gall bladder

Pancreas

HIDDEN PANCREAS

The pancreas is a long, yellowish organ that hides behind the stomach. It looks a bit like a strange, bumpy banana. The pancreas releases enzymes into the small intestine to help it break down food.

20

Breaks down poisons and medicines that enter the body.

Makes bile to send to the gall bladder.

Uses nutrients to build new chemicals that your body needs.

Holds a store of **vitamins** for your body to use.

THE CLEVER LIVER

Your liver, on the right side of your abdomen, is the biggest organ inside your body. It's very important for the digestive system, and does lots of other jobs too – more than 500 in all! Just a few of them are listed above.

Releases **hormones** that control the way you grow.

Catches and kills some types of germs.

YELLOW FELLOW!

When a person's liver isn't working properly, some of the chemicals it normally deals with may be released into the body. These chemicals make the skin and the whites of the eyes turn yellow.

Yellow eyes are a sign that your liver is unwell. This is a disease called jaundice.

IMAGINE THIS...

Sometimes, rock-hard, stone-like lumps called gallstones form in the gall bladder. They grow from chemicals in the bile and can be very painful.

Gallstones vary in size from the size of a grain of sand to the size of a golf ball!

WHAT IS FOOD USED FOR?

Food does lots of things for your body, such as helping you grow, repairing injuries and giving you energy to move around. Different kinds of food are useful for different jobs.

FOOD GROUPS

The main types of foods are called food groups. When your body digests food, it takes different nutrients from each food group. This is why a healthy diet includes many different foods. If you don't eat all of them, your body misses out on things it needs.

Many foods contain a combination of food groups. For example, an avocado contains fats, vitamins and fibre.

Carbohydrates are found in potatoes, pasta, bread, rice and other cereals. Sugar is also a carbohydrate. Carbohydrates are used as fuel to keep the body's **cells** working and muscles moving.

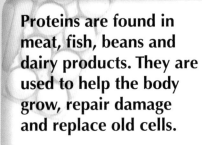

Proteins are found in meat, fish, beans and dairy products. They are used to help the body grow, repair damage and replace old cells.

22

Fibre is made of bits of food you can't digest, such as seed husks and vegetable skins. It helps sweep waste along your large intestine.

You need lots of water, or drinks containing water, to keep your body working. Water is used in blood, tears and sweat. It flows around the whole body. Every cell in your body needs water.

Minerals and vitamins are chemicals that you need in small amounts. Iron is a kind of mineral found in leafy vegetables and red meat. Vitamin C is a vitamin found in oranges and potatoes. These chemicals are used for many jobs – for example, blood needs iron in order to work.

Fats are found in oils, butter, nuts, and some types of meat, such as bacon. Fats are used as a fuel, and also help to keep the brain, skin and hair healthy.

Do I really have metals in my body?!

Yes! Your body contains enough iron to make a nail 2.5 cm long. Small amounts of other metals such as copper and zinc are also found in your body. You even contain a tiny bit of gold.

FOOD GROUP PIZZA

Pizza is sometimes seen as unhealthy, but that's only if you buy a takeaway pizza with too much salt and fat in it. At home, you can make a pizza that's really good for you and combines all the important food groups. Use the lists below to choose your toppings.

Carbohydrates

The pizza base provides the carbohydrates, as it's made of wheat, a type of cereal.

Fats

Cheese, olives, tuna, salmon, avocado

Vitamins

Vitamin B: Asparagus, eggs, turkey, chillis
Vitamin C: Tomato-based pizza sauce, red or green peppers
Vitamin D: Salmon, sardines
Vitamin E: Spinach, pine nuts, broccoli

Proteins

Cheese, chicken, beef, tuna, tofu, prawns

Minerals

Iron: Dried herbs, spinach, rocket
Copper: Squid, lobster, mushrooms
Zinc: Beef, prawns

Fibre

Pizza sauce, onions, pineapple, sweetcorn, aubergine

What are calories?

Calories are a measure of the energy or fuel in food. Calories aren't bad – you need energy. But if you have too many calories – by eating lots of high-calorie, fatty, sugary things – the energy gets stored as extra fat on your body. And that isn't good for you.

PIZZA RECIPE

To start, buy a ready-made thin-crust pizza base (or use a recipe book to make one). Choose your toppings so that they include a range of food groups. If you're using tomato sauce, that goes on first, then a sprinkling of cheese, and then the other toppings. Spread the toppings out evenly. When your pizza is ready, get an adult to help you to bake it in a hot oven for 10–15 minutes.

A slice of thin-crust pizza contains between about 130 and 200 calories. Two or three slices of your pizza will make a healthy meal.

GUT GUESTS

YIKES!

A human body is made up of about 10 trillion, or 10 million million (10,000,000,000,000) cells. But did you know that there are TEN TIMES as many cells living on and inside you – cells that aren't part of your body at all!

They are bacteria – tiny single-celled living things – that use our bodies as a home. Most of them are found in your guts, mainly in the large intestine, and are known as gut flora.

Don't panic! It's true that some types of bacteria can cause nasty diseases. But most of the bacteria in your guts are helpful. Humans, and many other animals, have adapted to share our bodies with bacteria. We give the gut flora a home and food. They help us by digesting food and turning it into useful nutrients.

Gut flora can make up as much as **3 per cent** of your body weight.

About 500 different kinds of bacteria live in your guts.

26

WASH YOUR HANDS!

Gut flora are helpful while living in your gut, but can make you ill if they are swallowed. That's why you have to wash your hands after going to the toilet, as some of the bacteria come out each time you go to the loo.

UNWELCOME GUESTS!

Sometimes living things that are not helpful, such as tapeworms, enter your guts. Tapeworms are **parasites**. They get into our bodies if we eat infected food containing their eggs. Once inside, they eat some of the food we've eaten. Luckily, we can get rid of them with worm-killing medicines. Phew!

PAAAARP!

As bacteria feed and digest food, they make gases as a waste product. These escape from our bottoms!

27

WASTE DISPOSAL

At the end of the digestive system, any leftovers need to leave the body. Your body stores the waste until you are ready to get rid of it by going to the toilet.

HOLDING AREA

Right at the end of the large intestine is an area called the rectum. Waste from the guts is stored here. When the rectum is full, it sends a signal to your brain, telling it that you'd better find a toilet soon. A strong ring of muscle called the anal sphincter holds everything in until you're ready to go! Finally, the **faeces** leave the body through the **anus** at the end of the rectum.

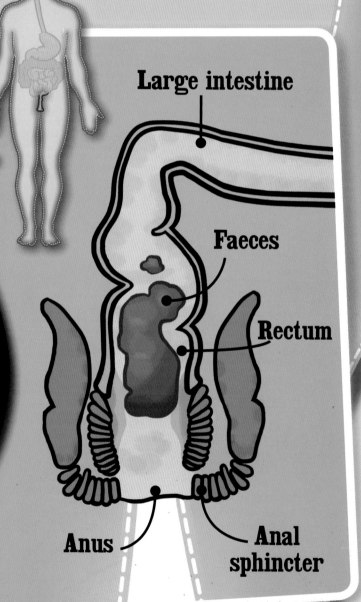

Large intestine

Faeces

Rectum

Anus

Anal sphincter

LIQUID WASTE

Your body makes liquid waste called **urine**, or wee. Urine is made up of water and waste chemicals collected by your blood from around your body. Two organs in your back, called kidneys, filter this waste out of the blood. The kidneys make a substance called urea, which mixes with water to form your wee. The wee is sent to be stored in a stretchy bag called the bladder. The bladder sends you a signal when it gets full, telling you it needs to be emptied.

What's in your wee?

Water (94%)

Urea (3.5%)

Salt (1%)

Other substances (1.5%)

Kidney

Blood vessels

Ureter
Tube leading to bladder

Bladder

Urethra
Tube leading out of body

Why should I drink water?

Drinking lots of water is very important for keeping your waste disposal systems healthy. This is because they use water to wash waste out. If there's not enough water in your body, the intestines and kidneys don't work as well.

29

COLLECT A DAY'S FOOD

This simple activity lets you see exactly what is moving through your digestive system by the end of the day.

YOU WILL NEED:
- Jam jar with a lid
- Fork
- Notebook or paper
- Teaspoon

1 Make sure your jar is washed out and dried. It needs to be ready when you wake up in the morning.

2 Keep the jar with you all day. When you eat or drink anything, use the teaspoon to collect some of it, and drop it into your jar. Use the fork to mash and break up solid foods.

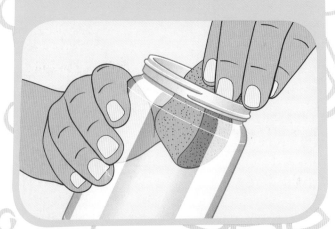

3 Each time you add some food or drink to the jar, screw the lid on tightly, then give it a good shake.

4 At bedtime, open the jar and have a good look! This is a small sample of what will be squeezing its way through your guts during the night.

Home cooking

It's easiest to do this experiment at a weekend, when you're mostly eating at home!

GLOSSARY

ABDOMEN
The central part of the body, also called the trunk or torso.

ANUS
Opening at the end of the large intestine, where poo leaves the body.

BACTERIA
Tiny living things that include some types of germs.

BLOOD VESSELS
Tubes that carry blood around the body.

CELLS
Tiny building blocks that make up the human body and other living things.

DIGEST
To break down food into nutrients and soak them up into the body.

DIGESTIVE SYSTEM
The set of organs and body parts that take in and digest food.

DISSOLVE
To change a solid into tiny parts that mix into a liquid.

ENZYMES
Chemicals that break down other substances into smaller parts.

FAECES
The scientific name for poo.

HORMONES
Chemicals that make changes happen in the body.

INTESTINES
Tubes that carry food from your stomach to the end of the digestive system.

MINERALS
Natural, non-living solid substances that the body needs in small amounts.

MUSCLE
A body part that contracts or squeezes to pull on other body parts.

NUTRIENTS
Chemicals found in food that are useful to the body.

ORGAN
A body part that does a particular job, such as the brain, heart or stomach.

PARASITE
A living thing that lives on or in another living thing and causes it harm.

URINE
Liquid body waste, also called wee.

VITAMINS
Chemicals that the body needs in small amounts.

INDEX